WI
CHRIS

By

HENRY DURBANVILLE

Published by

B. McCALL BARBOUR

28 George IV. Bridge

Edinburgh 1, Scotland

First published November, 1952
Reprinted October, 1953
Reprinted October, 1955
Reprinted April, 1960
Reprinted September, 1969
Reprinted in paperback – January, 1986

Cover picture by Whiteholme of Dundee

ISBN 0 7132 0032 4

Printed by Stanley L. Hunt (Printers) Ltd., Midland Road, Rushden, Northants

CONTENTS

" Character is consolidated habit, and
is ever tending to permanence "

JOSEPH COOK

FOREWORD

IN his volume *The Professor at the Breakfast Table,* Oliver Wendell Holmes asks this question : " Can any man look round and see what Christian countries are now doing, and how they are governed, and what is the general condition of society, without seeing that Christianity is the *flag* under which the world sails, and not the *rudder* that steers its course ? " That is an arresting question which, from the individual point of view, comes home to the heart of every Christian man and woman. For the time has arrived when the lives of Christians are about the only Bible which the world will read ; when what we are, has more weight than what we say ; when deeds speak more loudly than words. It cannot be too frequently affirmed that the final test of a man's Christianity is not in the sphere of opinion, or in that of professed belief ; but always and everywhere in the sphere of conscience and of love. Happy the Christian man whose manner of life gives validity and power to his message ; whose doctrine and whose life coincident, exhibit lucid proof that he is honest in the sacred cause.

Dr. S. D. Gordon mentions the four great tests of character.

First, the home test : how a man treats those with whom he lives.

Second, the business test : how a man conducts himself towards his customers and employees.

Third, the social test : how a man acts towards those who do not enjoy the same social advantages as himself.

Fourth, the success test : how a man behaves himself when favouring circumstances bring him wealth, power, position, and honour.

It is related of a great artist that he was wandering in the mountains of Switzerland, when some officials met him and demanded his passport. " I do not have it with me," he replied, " but my name is Doré ". " Prove it, if you are," replied the officers, knowing who Doré was, but not believing that this was he. Taking a piece of paper the artist hastily sketched a group of peasants who were standing near, and did it with such grace and skill that the officials exclaimed : " Enough, you are Doré ". The world cares little for mere profession ; but the man who emerges successfully from the fourfold test laid down by Dr. Gordon, carries the evidence of his genuineness with him. More and more one feels that our most earnest desire should be, not that of Balaam—" let me die the death of the righteous " ; but that of the modern writer who says : " Teach me to live, 'tis easier far to die ". It was because of this that Ernest Crosby wrote the poem which contains such heart-searching words :

" So he died for his faith. That is fine—
 More than most of us do.
But stay ! Can you add to that line
 That he lived for it, too ?

"It is easy to die. Men have died
For a wish or a whim—
From bravado or passion or pride.
Was it harder for him?

"But to live—every day to live out
All the truth that he dreamt,
While his friends met his conduct with doubt,
And the world, with contempt—

"Was it thus that he plodded ahead,
Never turning aside?
Then, we'll talk of the life that he led—
Never mind how he died."

INTRODUCTION

BEFORE we examine these traits of character which, as we have seen, speak more loudly than words, I desire to make it clear that all questions relative to our acceptance of Christ as Saviour, and our consequent acceptance by God in Him, are regarded as settled. We have learned that it is by the wondrous grace of God that we have washed our robes and made them white in the blood of the Lamb (Revelation 7); that it is by His unmerited favour that we have been saved through faith, and that, not of ourselves, it is the gift of God (Ephesians 2); that it is not by works of righteousness which we have done, but according to His mercy He saved us (Titus 3).

But we must also steadily bear in mind that the Book which declares that good works do not constitute salvation, just as definitely proclaims that they ought invariably to accompany salvation; that while they are not its procuring cause, they should always be its resulting consequence; that those who have been accepted *in* the Beloved, should henceforth labour strenuously to be acceptable *to* the Beloved (Ephesians 1. 6; 2nd Corinthians 5. 9, R.V.). Such will aim constantly at having a conscience void of offence toward God and man; and in lowliness of heart will seek day by day to manifest those lovely graces which are as really the evidence of faith, as flowers are the evidence of springtide. They work, not to the Cross, but from the Cross; not in order to be saved, but because they are saved. Having looked to God for salvation (Isaiah 45. 22), they now look to themselves, their ways, their acts, their lives, in order that they may ultimately merit the Master's "Well done" (2nd John, verse 8).

> "I would not work my soul to save,
> That work my Lord has done;
> But I'd fain work like any slave,
> For love to God's dear Son."

There are four great passages in the New Testament which set forth Christian character in all its winsomeness and power: Matthew 5. 3-12, with its nine beatitudes; 1st Corinthians 13, with its sixteen matchless qualities; Galatians 5. 22, 23, with its ninefold cluster of heavenly fruit; and 2nd Peter 1. 5-8, with its description of fully developed Christian manhood.

The words of Matthew 5 present a character schooled in humility, matured by suffering, instinct with gentleness, and purity, and love.

"First Corinthians 13 is," says Dean Alford, "perhaps the noblest assemblage of beautiful thoughts extant in this our world".

The paragraph in Galatians 5 unfolds the secret whereby we may have days of heaven upon earth.

Second Peter 1, assuming faith as the foundation, rises majestically, step by step, until the structure is crowned with that love which is the fulfilling of the Law.

Together, these four portions of the Bible set forth a complete and superb philosophy of Christian living; and we do well if, from time to time, we examine ourselves in the light of them. As a help in this direction, I suggest that we memorize them ; and that, besides our daily reading of the Word, we definitely set aside a portion of each Lord's Day for prolonged meditation on them.

CHAPTER I

THE DIGNITY OF UPRIGHTNESS

I PROPOSE now to select from the foregoing and other passages of the Scriptures, some of the things which will manifestly appear in the life of the man or woman who is guided by them ; and the first of these is Uprightness or Integrity.

The French have an expression *Noblesse Oblige,* which means that rank imposes obligation ; that, from those who claim lofty lineage and illustrious descent, conduct is expected in keeping with their claim. Children of the living God, heirs of the Kingdom, members of the royal family of Heaven, to you is the word of this exhortation sent. Uprightness, integrity, straight dealing before God and man : these are the essential things without which religious talk, eloquent prayers, and attendance at church or meeting, are valueless. It is not that a Christian cannot make mistakes, or fall short of the ideal. If you are looking for faultless men and women you had better go to the heavenly land right away ; for you will never find them here. But if a true Christian blunders, he will instantly own up to it ; for his aim is to reverence his conscience as his king. He never forgets that moral integrity is greater than intellectual eminence. Indeed, Paul reminds us (1st Corinthians 13. 1, 2), that the possession of outstanding academical gifts without that love which is the end of the commandment, turns a man into a thing that merely makes a noise.

President Lincoln was once approached by a man who wanted him to do a shady thing in business, and who urged the President to do it because, as he said, no one would know of it. " Yes," replied the great statesman, " Lincoln would know of it, and I have to sleep with him ". A Christian man, charged with malpractices, rose in a church meeting; and, stretching forth his hand, said: " That hand never gave a bribe, and never took a bribe ". " Gentlemen," said Joseph Reed when offered a bribe of ten thousand guineas to desert his country when she was fighting for her freedom: " Gentlemen, I am poor, very poor; but your king is not rich enough to buy me ". These incidents illustrate what should be the lifelong aim of every Christian man, namely, to possess an uncondemning heart, and to have a reputation for honest dealing in the affairs of life. If you are an employer you will delight to give good wages; if you are an employee you will find pleasure in giving good service.

The question has been asked: " Why are most rivers crooked? " And the reply is given: " A river becomes crooked when it follows the line of least resistance ". There will come times in your experience when it will be necessary to say, " No "; and there is tremendous power in that little word when it is spoken resolutely and courageously. It has often been like a giant rock by the sea, as it has encountered and hurled back the mighty waves of temptation. A Christian wrote recently from a country where God's people are sealing their testimony with their blood, and said: " Our prayer is this: 'Let me rather die a martyr's death, than live a life dishonouring to Thee' ". Religious freedom is disappearing from the earth ; and, even in our own favoured land, the time may come when unbending fidelity will cost us our lives. Should such a privilege be accorded us, pray God that we may quit ourselves like men.

This, then, is the first of the things that should characterize us as witnesses for our Lord. With deep humility of heart, but with head erect and soul ablaze, may we face the future unafraid—assured, as we are, that as our days, so shall our strength be—and that illimitable grace may be ours till travelling days are done (2nd Corinthians 9. 8).

Chapter II

THE BEAUTY OF COURTESY

COURTESY is like an air-cushion: there is nothing in it, but it eases the jolts of life. There is, however, another sense in which there is a great deal in it; for the supreme characteristic of courtesy is that thoughtfulness for others which is the very heart of Christianity. Schools of etiquette produce it by training; love does it by instinct.

I. The underlying thought in the New Testament use of the word is friendliness—(Acts 27. 3; 28. 7; 1st Peter 3. 8); and the daily round and common tasks of life give us endless opportunities of showing this. A man who was rushing along the street one night, violently collided with another who was hurrying out of a doorway. The latter was infuriated, and used abusive language; but the first man, politely removing his hat, said: "I don't know which of us is to blame for this encounter, and I am in too great a hurry to find out. If I ran into you, I beg your pardon; if you ran into me, don't mention it". An answer like that wins respect and conciliates antagonism.

II. A courteous man will never knowingly hurt or wound the feelings of another. A fine example of courtesy was given by King Edward VII some years ago. The French President, M. Fallieres, was making a State visit to England; and the King gave instructions that the train bringing the

President should not arrive at Waterloo Station, and that the route of his carriage should avoid Trafalgar Square. Both of these names held unpleasant memories for a Frenchman, and the monarch, in this thoughtful way, obviated the recalling of them. Louis XIV, telling a story before his courtiers at Versailles, suddenly ended it very flatly. A few minutes after, a prince left the room. The King then said : " You must have noticed how lamely my story ended. I forgot that it reflected on an ancestor of the Prince who has just left the room ; and I thought it better to spoil a good story than to distress a good man ". Courtesy—that gentle refinement and grace of manner—will lead a man to be respectful to superiors, polite to equals, kind to inferiors. It is a diamond which, whether set in gold or in the rough, is of great value.

III. A man usually reveals himself in his private letters ; and in the only personal letter which we have of the apostle Paul—the epistle to Philemon—we see how courteous a gentleman he was. Of it Rabbi Duncan says : " The most gentlemanly letter ever written, by the most perfect gentleman, is, in my opinion, Paul's epistle to Philemon. If you study its courtesies, you will see how manifold and how delicate they are ".

If you want to see how Paul asks a favour, read the epistle to Philemon ; if you want to see how he returns thanks, read the epistle to the Philippians (chapter 4. 10-21).

If we all resolve that henceforth we will be gentle, courteous, thoughtful, unobtrusively sympathetic, and persistently friendly, how many unpleasant things will be obviated !

Chapter III

THE WINSOMENESS OF KINDNESS

THE Bible speaks much of Kindness—this beautiful trait of character. It has words which reveal the loving-kindness of God to us—(Titus 3. 3-7; Luke 6. 35; Isaiah 54. 10); and exhortations to show kindness to one another—(Romans 12. 10; Ephesians 4. 32; 2nd Peter 1. 5-7).

I. Definition of kindness

Kindness is the latest flower of love; the last rose of the heart's summer. It is not revealed in great world-shaking deeds, but in those little nameless acts of love that constitute the best portion of a good man's life.

II. The great need for kindness

"Next to bread," says someone, "the greatest longing of the human heart is for kindness". "Be kind," says another, "for every man is fighting a hard battle". "The greatest thing we can do for our Heavenly Father," says a third, "is to be kind to some of His children". "I wonder," says a great writer, "why it is that we are not all kinder than we are? How much the world needs it! How easily it is done! How instantaneously it acts! How infallibly it is remembered! How superabundantly it pays itself back!" There is a quaint extract from an old book which carries its own lesson with it. "There came unto Shakum one who read the Pyramids like a book, and was almost certain as to the exact date of the end of the world. And he explained unto Shakum that whilst he knew all these things, he feared that his family hated him. And Shakum, having agreed with him that this probably was so, urged him in future, beginning with his own family, to try to cure fevered humanity, not so much with the barometer of prophecy, as with the thermometer of sympathy. And when he began to do this, everyone was much happier."

III. The tragedy of post-mortem kindness

"Then took Mary a pound of ointment of spikenard, very costly, and anointed the feet of Jesus, and wiped His feet with her hair; and the house was filled with the odour of the ointment" (John 12. 3). "After this Joseph of Arimathæa, being a disciple of Jesus, but secretly for fear of the Jews, besought Pilate that he might take away the body of Jesus. . . . And there came also Nicodemus . . . and brought a mixture of myrrh and aloes, about an hundred pound weight" (John 19. 38, 39). These two scriptures are set in contrast. The first tells of the devotion of a loving heart, that expressed itself when the Saviour was alive; the second, of devotion that was shown to our Lord after He was dead. Mary's gift weighed one pound; Nicodemus' gift weighed one hundred pounds. Some have wondered if he tried to make up for the lateness of his tribute, by its largeness. The one shows the helpfulness of timely kindness; the other, the futility of post-mortem kindness.

There are heart lessons here for us all. "Do not

keep the alabaster boxes of your love and tenderness sealed up until your friends are dead. Fill their lives with sweetness. Speak approving, cheering words while their ears can hear them, and while their hearts can be thrilled and made happier by them ; the kind things you mean to say when they are gone, say before they go. The flowers you mean to send for their coffins, send to brighten and sweeten their homes before they leave them." One thinks of the heart-moving words of Robert Meyers :

" O friends, I pray tonight,
Keep not your kisses for my dead cold brow ;
The way is lonely ; let me feel them now.
Think gently of me ; I am travel-worn ;
My faltering feet are pierced with many a thorn ;
Forgive, O hearts estranged, forgive I plead !
When dreamless rest is mine I shall not need
The tenderness, for which I long tonight."

IV. Conclusion

A little kindness goes much further than a great deal of religiosity. " Let, therefore," says John Ruskin, " every dawn of morning be to you as the beginning of life, and every setting sun be to you as its close. Let every one of these short lives leave its sure record of some kindly thing done for others ".

CHAPTER IV

THE GREATNESS OF HUMILITY

THE word Humility is derived from *humus*—the ground—and is the equivalent of the Saxon word, *lowliness*. It is synonymous with *modesty*, and means, not underestimating, but correctly estimating ourselves. " By *humility* we do not intend the servility which crouches, or the meanness that creeps, or the sycophancy which fawns ; but a disposition to think lowly of our attainments, a tendency to dwell upon our defects rather than our excellencies, an apprehension of our inferiority compared with those around us, with what we ought to be, and what we might be. It is always attended with that modest deportment, which neither boasts of itself, nor seeks to depreciate anyone : humility is the inward feeling of lowliness—modesty is the outward expression of it ; humility leads a man to feel that he deserves little—modesty leads him to demand little."

I. The humble man has a lowly opinion of himself

The beloved Jonathan Brierley used to say to himself each morning : " Brierley, you old sinner, you get heaps better than your deserts ". Copernicus, the great mathematician, directed that the following inscription be placed on his tombstone : " I do not ask a kindness equal to that given to Paul ; nor do I ask the grace granted to Peter ;

but that forgiveness which Thou didst grant to the robber—that, earnestly, I crave ". A young college student had a card in his room bearing the inscription: " I am willing to be third ". When pressed to tell the meaning, he refused for a while, but after a time said, " My mother taught me to put Christ first, others second, and self last; so I am willing to be third ".

II. The humble man is saved from many sorrows

Did we but know the perils which surround those who occupy high positions, we would cease envying them and commence praying for them—thankful and content to fill, in lowly obscurity, the niche which God intends us to fill.

" . . . As the storm that makes
The high elm crouch and rends the oak,
The humble lily spares—so, a thousand blows
That shake the lofty Monarch on his throne
We lesser folk feel not. Keen are the pains
Advancement often brings. To be secure
Be humble; to be happy be content."

III. God giveth grace to the humble man (James 4. 6)

" Of all trees, I observe that God hath chosen the vine, a low plant that creeps upon the helpful wall; of all beasts, the soft and patient lamb; of all fowls, the mild and guileless dove. Christ is the rose of the field and the lily of the valley. When God appeared to Moses, it was not in the lofty cedar, nor the sturdy oak, nor the spreading palm; but in a bush, a humble, slender, abject shrub; as if He would, by these elections, check the conceited arrogance of man."

" He that is down need fear no fall,
He that is low, no pride ;
He that is humble ever shall
Have God to be his guide."

Chapter V

THE EXCELLENCE OF TRUSTWORTHINESS

If there is one thing more than another that wins the respect of good men and women everywhere, it is the grace of Trustworthiness. This fine trait of character is the foundation of all true friendship, the basis of all successful enterprise, the groundwork of all confidence between man and man. Such confidence is not won in a day: it is the result of long years of patient continuance in well doing; and I mention three methods by which it may be secured.

I. Be true to those who trust you

When Alexander the Great lay seriously ill of a fever, Philip, his medical adviser, prescribed a remedy, and offered it to him. But just then a letter was handed to Alexander accusing Philip of treason and of designs to poison him. Such, however, was his confidence in his physician that, when he had read it, he with one hand quietly handed the letter to Philip, and with the other raised the draught to his lips and drank it off. The sequel proved that his confidence was not misplaced, for he speedily recovered. The physician had been true.

II. Be conscientious in small things

Luke 16. 10 makes it clear that morality is not a thing of magnitude, but of quality; and, since

" character is consolidated habit and is ever tending to permanence ", the habit of being faithful in small things when one is young, will be the best preservative against that deterioration of character which sometimes overtakes men in middle life. Whether you are appointed treasurer of the cricket club, or of the missionary society, carefully record and account for all money entrusted to your care. Faithfulness here will equip you for the larger tasks that will come later on.

Since all service ranks the same with God, the principle applies to every detail of life. As saith the poet :

> " If I were a cobbler, I'd make it my pride,
> The best of all cobblers to be.
> If I were a tinker, no tinker beside,
> Should mend an old kettle like me."

III. Be loyal to your promises

" There are all sorts of men who have been praised for all sorts of things. But I give first place, first prize, and the blue ribbon, also honourable mention, the gold medal, and the Victoria Cross, together with the Nobel Prize, and three cheers, to the man who keeps his word."

CHAPTER VI

THE HELPFULNESS OF PUNCTUALITY

THE word Punctuality is derived from a Latin word which signifies " a point ". The punctual man is the man who is prompt to a very tittle, and careful to a very point. At the hour appointed he will be at his post.

A Christian man should be punctual in the discharge of every business appointment; for late arrival for an engagement may upset a busy person's timetable. Some time ago a committee of eight ladies, who managed the affairs of an institution which had been formed for the relief of the poor, agreed to meet on a certain day, at twelve o'clock. Seven of them were present at the appointed hour; the eighth did not arrive till a quarter of an hour after. She came in and said: " I am very sorry to be behind the appointed time, but really the time slipped away without my being sensible of it: I hope your goodness will excuse it ". A member replied: " Had thyself only lost a quarter of an hour, it would have been merely thine own concern; but in this case the quarter must be multiplied by eight, as we each lost a quarter; so that there have been two hours of useful time sacrificed by thy want of punctuality ". Because late arrival at a religious meeting may disturb the thoughts of the other worshippers, it is well to form the habit of getting to church or meeting, a few minutes before the appointed hour. Failure here has led someone to suggest that another verse should be added to the old hymn :

> " Get up, get up for Jesus,
> Ye soldiers of the Cross ;
> A lazy Sunday morning
> Means certain harm and loss ;
> If Christians, on a week-day,
> Begin their work at seven,
> They surely can, on Sunday,
> Start worship at eleven."

On answering letters

One mark of Mr. Gladstone's courtesy was the extraordinary promptness with which he answered letters. Ian Maclaren, on the other hand, complains very bitterly of some of his colleagues in this regard. Urgent letters, which it would have taken the recipient only two or three minutes to deal with, were left unanswered for weeks—upsetting his work, and creating a good deal of ill feeling. I counsel youthful readers of this book to get into the habit of dealing with business letters by return of post if possible, and to be prompt in acknowledging gifts, or letters that confer favours.

One exception to this rule, however, is the letter that annoys or irritates you. Unless it is essential to deal with it immediately, put it in your drawer for three days before you answer it. The reply which you are likely to give after that time will be the correct one.

Chapter VII

THE HARMFULNESS OF DEFAMATION

I. *The danger*

"At two things I am growingly amazed," said Dr. Jowett, on one occasion; "first, at the solemnity with which the Bible warns against the sins of slander and of evil speaking; and second, at the lightness with which many Christian people indulge them". There is scarcely anything in the Word of God to parallel the severity of the language which it employs about the misuse of the tongue. It is compared to the spark which sets the vast forest in flames; to the rudder which, by a false turn, can send the mighty man-of-war crashing on the rocks; to the poison which contaminates the whole body; to the ferocious animal which no man can tame (James 3. 4-8).

Now, the true Christian will not only utter no slander; he will not even listen to it. He will refuse to take up a reproach against his neighbour (Psalm 15. 3). If a person who has a reputation for talebearing comes to you with a rumour about some friend, you are immediately confronted with the duty of being true to yourself, to your friend, to the slanderer, and to your God. Before you allow him to speak, remind him that your Master has counselled you to take heed *what* you hear (Mark 4. 24); and ask him two questions: "Will it be a help to your absent friend that you should hear this report?" and "will it be for the glory of God?"

Assuming now, however, that you have been told something detrimental of another, your duty is clearly described in Deuteronomy 13. 12-14; a scripture which reveals how eminently fair God would have us be to those about whom a report is circulated. He tells His people that if they shall hear say that certain men are introducing idolatry into the land, they are (1) *to enquire*; (2) *to make search*; (3) *to ask diligently*. If, after thorough investigation, they find that it be truth, and the thing certain that such abomination is wrought among them—then, and only then, were they to take action. How many broken hearts and ruined homes would have been saved if this heavenly counsel had always been followed! Hannah More had a good way of dealing with talebearers. Whenever she was told anything that was derogatory of another, her invariable reply was: "Come, we will go and ask if this be true". The effect was sometimes ludicrously painful. The talebearer was taken aback, stammered out a qualification, or begged that no notice might be taken of the statement. But the good lady was inexorable; off she took the scandalmonger to the scandalized to make inquiry and compare accounts. It is not likely that anybody ever a second time ventured to repeat a gossipy story to Hannah More.

But what if the report is true? Even if it be true, by repeating it unnecessarily you violate the law of Christian love. Listen to this:

"If you are tempted to reveal
  A tale told to you by someone
About another, make it pass,
  Before you speak, three gates of gold.

Three narrow gates : first, Is it true ?
  Then, Is it needful ? In your mind
Give truthful answer. And the next
  Is last and narrowest—Is it kind ?
And if to reach your lips at last,
  It passes through these gateways three,
Then you may tell the tale, nor fear
  What the results of speech may be."

II. The Remedy

The first thing to recognize is that we are up against a task which, in our own strength, we cannot fulfil. "The tongue can no man tame." But what man cannot do, God can do ; and, yielding ourselves afresh to His sway, I suggest that we each seek some quiet spot where we shall be alone with Him, and where we shall unhurriedly take the following resolves :

(a) *Never to speak evil of any man* (*Titus* 3. 2).

In reflections on the absent, go no further than you would go if they were present. When Plato forsook Syracuse for the last time, disgusted with the unmanliness and cruelty of Dionysius the younger, the tyrant, apprehensive for his reputation in Greece said : "I suppose, Plato, that when you return to your companions in the Academy, my faults will often be the subject of your censure ?" To which the great philosopher replied : "I hope, Dionysius, that we shall never be at such a loss for a subject as to mention them at all".

(b) *In our Christian fellowships, sternly to discourage the known slanderer and retailer of gossip.*

On the table in Augustine's home these lines were

inscribed : " Whoever delights to slander the absent, let him know that this table is forbidden to him ".

(c) *Always to cultivate kindly thoughts of everybody.*

" Don't look for flaws as you go through life,
And even when you find them,
It is wise and kind to be somewhat blind,
And look for the virtues behind them."

When a man measures himself in the presence of God, and when he looks at his fellow pilgrims through the eyes of the Master, he will feel as Stevenson felt when he said : " There is so much that is good in the worst of us, and so much that is bad in the best of us, that it ill behoves any one of us to speak any ill of the rest of us ".

First Corinthians 13, the great chapter on Love, presents a positive cure for all the unlovely things of which we have been thinking. Let us read it frequently on our knees. Let us make Psalm 141. 3 our daily prayer ; and Psalm 34. 1 our daily practice.

CHAPTER VIII

THE GRANDEUR OF EQUANIMITY

THE self-mastery of which the Scriptures speak, includes control of the thoughts, of the tongue, and of the temper. It is of the last named of these that we are now to speak. The outstanding illustration of the evil effects of giving way to anger, is Moses. Although, because of his loyalty to God and truth he renounced the throne of Egypt (Hebrews 11. 24-26); although he was faithful in all his house (Hebrews 3. 5); and although he was the meekest man in all the earth at that time (Numbers 12. 3); yet this mighty man of God tripped and fell in the last lap of the race. "He spake unadvisedly with his lips," a failure which cost him Canaan (Psalm 106. 32, 33).

The book of Proverbs has a good deal to say about this matter. It says that the man who readily goes off at the deep end is a fool (chapter 12. 16); that, on the other hand, he that is slow to wrath is of great understanding (chapter 14. 29); that, indeed, such a man is greater than he who achieves great military victories (chapter 16. 32). Peter the Great, although one of the mightiest of the Czars of Russia, failed here. In a fit of temper he struck his gardener, and a few days afterwards the gardener died. "Alas," said Peter, sadly, "I have conquered other nations, but I have not been able to conquer myself".

The most effective way by which this and every

other short-coming can be overcome, however, is by what Dr. Chalmers calls " the expulsive power of a new affection ". Dr. F. B. Meyer records that at a meeting in the house of Wilberforce, many were telling their experiences of how they were tempted and prayed to be delivered ; whereupon an old clergyman said : " I have listened to those who have spoken of the conditions in which they prayed for help : I think I have learned something different. I was speaking to a number of children one hot Sunday afternoon ; and finding that the flowers and birds outside were attracting them, and they wanted to get away, and that I was fast losing my patience, I turned to Christ and said : ' Lord, my patience is giving out ; grant me Thine ; ' and He dropped into my heart a lump of patience, and I could then stand twice as much noise and disturbance ".

Meeting Dr. Meyer next morning, Mr. Wilberforce said : " What did you think of that ? "—to which Dr. Meyer replied : " It has changed my life. Henceforth, instead of conflicting with temptation, I claim the opposite ; not simply refusing, resisting, fighting, but taking, in the moment of impurity, His purity ; in the moment of anxiety, His direction and wisdom ".

" He giveth more grace when the burdens grow greater;
He sendeth more strength when the labours increase;
To added affliction He addeth His mercy,
To multiplied trials, His multiplied peace.

" When we have exhausted our store of endurance,
When our strength has failed ere the day is half done,
When we reach the end of our hoarded resources,
OurFather's full giving is only begun.

' His love has no limit, His grace has no measure,
  His power no boundary known unto men ;
For out of His infinite riches in Jesus
  He giveth, and giveth, and giveth again."

Of similar import is the message of Amy Carmichael. When tempted to utter a flashing retort, she said to herself : " See in this a chance to die " ; and as she turned to commune with the risen Lord, the temptation to read the riot act disappeared. " There is one admonition ever in place, not exactly in Scripture language, but absolutely in line with its spirit—*keep sweet.* It is well for the Christian to make it the rule of his life, under all circumstances, in all duties, in all vexations, in all trials and grievances, and privations and sorrows, and in all and through all, to *keep sweet.* Everyone engaging in any sort of business will find daily trials. There will be need of patience. There will be many difficulties. Men will come short. There will be those who disappoint, and those who seek to take advantage of you. Do not let them rob you of your true dignity, and repose of spirit. In patience possess ye your souls. You will do but little that will have paid you for the doing, if it rob you of your peace and quietness of heart. And so, in all your daily work and duties, *keep sweet.*"

Chapter IX

THE NOBILITY OF MERCIFULNESS

WEYMOUTH'S translation of 1st Corinthians 13. 5 is : " Love does not brood over wrongs " ; Moffatt's, " It is never resentful " ; while the R.V. rendering is : " Love taketh not account of evil ". These indicate that Love never bears any malice.

An outstanding illustration of this occurred in England some years ago. When William Ewart Gladstone was Chancellor of the Exchequer, he sent down to the Treasury for certain statistics upon which to base his budget proposals. The statistician made a mistake. But Gladstone was so sure of this man's accuracy that he did not take time to verify his figures. He went before the House of Commons and made his speech, basing his appeal on the incorrect figures that had been given him. His speech was no sooner published than the newspapers exposed its glaring inaccuracies.

Mr. Gladstone was naturally overwhelmed with embarrassment. He went to his office and sent at once for the statistician who was responsible for his humiliating situation. The man came full of fear and shame, certain that he was going to lose his position. But, instead, Gladstone said : " I know how much you must be disturbed over what has happened, and I have sent for you to put you at your ease. For a long time you have been engaged in handling the intricacies of the national accounts, and this is the first mistake that you have made. I want to congratulate you, and express to you my keen appreciation ". It took a big man to do that, big with the bigness of the truly merciful.

The worst of men do not so much need our forgiveness, as the best of men need the forgiveness of God ; and one would have thought that the wonderful mercy shown to us by our gracious Father, would make the forgiving of our brother man for any injury he may have done to us, a very simple matter. But Matthew 18. 21-35 stands before us as an awful warning in this regard. Dr. Boreham gives an appalling instance of the results of an unforgiving spirit. " Many years ago," he says, " I visited an old man during an illness. He was a man whom nobody liked—hard, sullen, taciturn, and sour. If you met him on the street and wished him ' Good-day ', he would keep his eyes straight in front of him, grunt sulkily and pass on. He lived in a tumbled-down old hut away back in the bush. He spoke to nobody, and he made it perfectly plain that he wished nobody to speak to him. Even the children shunned him.

" Some said he was a hermit ; some that he was a miser ; some that he was a woman-hater ; some that he was a fugitive from justice—a man with a guilty secret. But they were all wrong. The simple truth was that in his youth, a companion had done him a grievous injury. ' I'll remember it to my dying day,' he hissed, in a gust of passionate resentment.

" And he did. But when his dying day actually came, he realized that the rankling memory of that youthful wrong had soured and darkened his whole life. ' I've gone over it by myself every morning,' he moaned, as he lay gasping in his comfortless shanty, ' and I've thought of it every night. I see now,' he added brokenly—a suspicion of moisture glistening in his eye—' that my bitterness has eaten out my soul. My hate has hurt nobody but myself. But God knows, it's turned my life into hell! ' It was true.

" The man at whom he had spat out his venomous maledictions, having done all a man could do to atone for the suffering that he had thoughtlessly caused, had dismissed the matter from his mind, a generation back. Upon him my gnarled old friend's bitterness had produced little or no effect. It was the man who cherished the sinister memory who suffered most. It shadowed his life; it lent a new terror to death; it expelled every ray of hope; and, at last, a grim and ghostly companion, it lay down with him in his cold and cheerless grave."

Let us beware! The wrath that sees two suns is condemned by Scripture (Ephesians 4. 26).

But Christianity never stops at negatives. Not only does it inculcate forgiveness till seventy times seven, it urges the positive heaping of blessings on the one who does the injury. The Irishman's method of getting even with an enemy illustrates the fact that the perpetrator of revenge suffers more than the victim of it. " Do you know that fellow Moriarity that is always comin' up and thumpin' ye on the chest and shoutin', ' How are ye '? " " I know him, Pat." " He's made me ache more than once—but I'll get even with him now! " " How will ye do that? " " I'll tell ye. He always hits me over my right vest pocket. He'll hit me just once more. I've put a stick of dynamite in that vest pocket." No, no, Pat, old chap, this will never do. Let me show you a more excellent way :

" The best revenge is love ; disarm
Anger with smiles ; heal wounds with balm ;
Give water to thy thirsty foe.
  The sandal tree, as if to prove
  How sweet to conquer hate by love,
Perfumes the axe that lays it low."

" Draw the curtain of night upon injuries," says Bacon ; " shut them up in the tower of oblivion, and let them be as though they had not been ".

CHAPTER X

THE ATTRACTIVENESS OF CHEERFULNESS

CHEERFULNESS—the bright weather of the heart—consists in that happy frame of mind which is best described by its negation of all that pertains to what is morbid, sombre, and morose. Its perfection is displayed in general good temper, united to much kindliness of heart. A life without it is a Lapland winter without a sun.

It would seem that cheerfulness among Christians is regarded by some folk as a very rare thing. Some years ago an advertisement appeared in an English paper reading as follows: "Wanted: an elderly man to live indoors; must be a Christian; cheerful if possible"! But surely, surely, Alexander Raleigh is nearer the truth when he says: "When I know that I have a Father in heaven Who watches over me, Who forgives my sin, Who strengthens every holy purpose in me, provides for all my needs, cares for me in all my cares, supports and guides me . . . and draws me towards His heart and home, why should I not be cheerful as my life is long?"

I. Cheerfulness versus Mirth

"I have always preferred cheerfulness to mirth," says Addison. "The latter I consider as an act; the former as a habit of the mind. . . . Mirth is like a flash of lightning that breaks through a gloom of clouds, and glitters for a moment; cheerfulness keeps up a kind of daylight in the mind, and fills it with a steady and perpetual serenity." The ideal here is cheerfulness without levity, seriousness without gloom.

II. Moods are capable of discipline

Do we recognize the force of will in regulating the soul's moods? These latter can unquestionably be trained. While it requires more than mere resolution to fill the life with joy, the exercise of the will can arrest the tendency to get depressed, and gloomy, and sad, as the following Scriptures show: Psalms 43. 5; 61. 4; 104. 34.

III. What cheerfulness will do

"A cheerful temper, joined with innocence, will make beauty attractive, knowledge delightful, and wit good-natured. Persons who are always innocently cheerful and good-humoured are very useful in the world; they maintain peace and happiness, and spread a thankful temper amongst all who live around them." A physician of Philadelphia left his house one morning, and was hurrying down the street, when he noticed a peculiar and ferocious-looking man, whose gaze was fastened upon him. Being one of the most kind and polite of men, he smiled gently, raised his hat, and passed on, when suddenly he heard a shot. Turning, he found that the stranger had just left his home with the insane purpose of killing the first man he met. He was the first man, but his kind face and benign smile had thrown the man off his guard, and the next passer-by had caught the bullet intended for him. That smile and bow saved his life.

Chapter XI

THE CHARM OF GENTLEMANLINESS

"ONCE a Christian, always a gentleman." This old saying indicates the high standard that is set for all who name the name of Christ; and although we may be conscious of having come short of it, we do well to keep it always before us. The Christian, indeed, should be the highest type of gentleman. Although he may not be able to boast of noble descent, or of having received a classical education, he learns in the school of grace, where the heart keeps pace with the head, lessons that will enable him to bear, without abuse, the grand old name of "Gentleman." Among the many fine things that characterize him, I name four.

I. He is careful to cultivate good manners

It is the most natural thing for him to stand, in vehicles, for aged people, and to avoid pushing in crowds. "I like her, because she looks as though she didn't see the holes in my shoes," said a little boy, of a lady. And of another it was said:

"She never found fault with you, never implied
Your wrong by her right: and yet men at her side
Grew nobler, girls purer, and through the whole town
The children were gladder that pulled at her gown."

II. He is above doing a mean thing

He is generous and brave, and never descends to anything that is dishonourable. He invades no secrets in the keeping of another. He betrays none confined to his own keeping. He never stabs in the dark. He is not one thing to a man's face, and another behind his back. He has a cheer for those who pass him in the race. His mind is filled with the things that are true, honourable, just, pure, lovely, and of good report ; and the opposites of these things have no place in his life (Philippians 4. 8).

III. He will never willingly give pain

Conscious of the sense of tears in things mortal, a true gentleman does not make life hard for anyone. " So long as I have been here," said Lincoln, after his second election, " I have not willingly planted a thorn in any man's bosom ". Someone has defined a gentleman as " one who never puts his feelings before the rights of others ; or his rights before their feelings ".

IV. He has a touch of kindly humour

" God made both tears and laughter, and both for kind purposes. For, as laughter enables mirth and surprise to breathe freely, so tears enable sorrow to vent itself patiently. Tears hinder sorrow from becoming despair and madness ; and laughter is one of the privileges of reason, being confined to the human species." These two things form part of the universal language of the human race—the language of looks. Since Babel, men in different parts of the world do not understand one another's speech ; but this one inarticulate language is understood everywhere. The newly born babe seems to bring some understanding of it with him into the world ; the black man may read it in the face of the white man.

The wise man affirms that a merry heart maketh a cheerful countenance, and doeth good like a medicine (Proverbs 15. 13 ; 17. 22). What is more refreshing than the merry laugh of a child ? It is the bubbling up of the fountain of innocence and simplicity in the little one's heart. Did not our Master bid us to become as little children ?

" Be assured then that you will make your own life happier and better, and through your happiness the lives of others happier and better, by using the faculty of humour to heal dissensions, to solve anger, to mitigate suffering, to cheer adversity, to save us from the wearing action of petty troubles, to arm us with the brightness of spirit which makes the best, and not the worst, of everything ! "

CHAPTER XII

THE USEFULNESS OF DOING GOOD

" This is a faithful saying, and these things I will that thou affirm constantly, that they which have believed in God might be careful to maintain good works. These things are good and profitable unto men " (*Titus* 3. 8).

IT has been said that usefulness is the rent which is due from us for being allowed to live in this world ; and, lest any of us are in arrears with our payments, I desire now that we examine together the place which good works hold in the economy of Grace. That they do hold a place in that economy your concordance of the Bible will immediately show you ; and if the old axiom—that the amount of space, devoted in Scripture to the exposition of any given theme, is the criterion of its importance—be a true one, then it behoves us to look into this matter very carefully indeed ; for this subject holds a prominent place in the New Testament.

I. The first thing we learn is that although good works can never purchase salvation, they ought always to appear in the life of the one who has received salvation

" Do you believe in good works, Mr. Spurgeon ? ", the great preacher was once asked. " Yes," he replied, " and I also believe in chimney tops ; but I do not believe in making chimney tops the foundation of the house ". That is a quaint way of explaining an aspect of this subject that is vital to its proper understanding. For no one so sternly opposes good works, performed with a view to meriting salvation, as does the apostle Paul; and no one so strenuously insists upon the absolute necessity for them, as evidence of salvation received, as does he. He tells us, on the one hand, that "to him that worketh not, but believeth on Him that justifieth the ungodly, his faith is counted for righteousness" (Romans 4. 5); that it is by grace we are saved through faith, and that not of ourselves, it is the gift of God (Ephesians 2. 8-9); that it is "not by works of righteousness which we have done, but according to His mercy He saved us" (Titus 3. 5).

On the other hand, his writings abound with exhortations to the people of God to see that their lives are filled with good works and kindly deeds. He tells us that we are His workmanship, created in Christ Jesus unto good works, which God has prepared that we should walk in them (Ephesians 2. 10, R.V.); that we are to be zealous of good works (Titus 2. 14); that we are to be fruitful in every good work, and ever increasing in the knowledge of God (Colossians 1. 10). It is thus made clear that while good works are no substitute for faith in the Redeemer, they form a necessary part of a well-ordered Christian life.

II. The second thing we learn is that doing good is not limited to the mere giving of money

If it were, some of earth's favoured ones could do good with the greatest ease, while others would be shut out from the privilege altogether. The noblest, the only perfect Man that this world has ever seen, was one of its poorest. He frequently, in life, had nowhere to lay His head; and when He died they placed Him in a borrowed tomb. Yet, of Him it is written that He went about doing good (Acts 10. 38). He fed and healed the bodies of men, as well as preached to them the glad tidings of redeeming grace; comforted sorrowing hearts, as well as announced the message of pardon to guilty ones; and we do well to follow His steps. Your contribution to the Master's interests on the earth may be that of lifting those who have fallen by the wayside, of inspiring with fresh hope those who have been worsted in the battle of life, of lavishing the affection of a sympathetic heart on those who live in the deep valleys of shadowland.

Having made it clear that the giving of gold is by no means the only way of doing good to the children of men, I desire now to emphasize that, with the blessing of heaven, the bestowing of money can be one of the most effective methods of carrying out this ministry. It is for this reason that Paul says to the young pastor, Timothy: "Charge them that are rich in this world, that they be not highminded, nor trust in uncertain riches, but in the living God, Who giveth us richly all things to enjoy; that they do good, that they be rich in good works, ready to distribute, willing to communicate" (1st Timothy 6. 17, 18). One Monday morning a man said to a servant of God: "That was a fine sermon on Heaven which you preached last night, Pastor; but you did not tell us where Heaven is". "Didn't I, man?" said the preacher. "Well, I am glad to have the opportunity of doing so now. Look, my brother," he continued, "do you see that little cottage on the hillside yonder? In that cottage there is a poor widow with little children, and there is neither food nor fuel in the house. I want you to go to the grocer now, order a sovereign's worth of foodstuffs and fuel, take them to that poor woman, and ask her kindly to accept them in the name of the Lord. Then, I want you to read to her the 23rd Psalm, and to pray with her. And if, by the time you get through with that little job, you do not find out where Heaven is, I will pay for the groceries myself". Next day the two men met again; and, with a radiant face the one said: "Pastor, I was in Heaven yesterday, and spent some time there".

A great Scottish physician visiting Paris was asked by a lady to call on a sick man in a side street. Acquiescing, the doctor went and saw the man, whom he found to be a fellow-countryman. Realizing that he needed food more than medicine, he got a pill box, filled it with golden sovereigns, and wrote on it: "One to be taken as required". Oh, the luxury of doing good!

A rich farmer, during his prayer at family worship one day, petitioned God long and earnestly that help for their bodily needs might be sent to a poor family living nearby. His small son was observed to be in deep thought afterwards, and at last he ran to his father with a bright face. "Daddy," said the child, "you can answer your prayer for the poor Smiths, yourself, can't you?" That is a modern interpretation and a very pungent application of the great passage in the epistle of James: chapter 2. 14 to 18. "My little children," says the loving-hearted John, "let us not love in word, neither in tongue ; but in deed and in truth " (1st John 3. 18). From this we learn that emotional fervour and eloquent expressions are of little value ; but, that practical deeds are of vital importance.

III. Doing good to others has reflex values for the doer

When we cease to hold the balance between the culture of the inner life, and loving ministry to our fellow-men, we become a prey to the wild beasts of morbidity and depression, of despondency and gloom. Master Eckhart, one of the exponents of the spiritual life, who lived in the thirteenth century, said that if a man were enjoying a state of rapture such as Paul records, and he heard of someone who was hungry, he would be justified in breaking off his spiritual enjoyment, and in taking a cup of soup to the hungry man. Such a man—one who forgets himself in the interests of others—will never be a loser. " When I dig a man out of a hole," says someone, " the pit, from which I lift him, becomes a grave where I bury my own sorrows ". A story is told of two Alpine travellers who were caught in a terrible snowstorm. As they descended, weary and benumbed with the intense cold, they came upon the unconscious form of another traveller, who had been completely overcome, and was lying in the snow. They knew that if he were left to lie there it meant death ; yet they were anxious to reach a place of safety before being themselves overcome. " We cannot save him, let us look after ourselves," said one, and hurried on. The other remained ; and, half-numbed though he was, began to rub and chafe the frozen hands and feet of the senseless traveller until the unfortunate one began slowly to revive. The exercise sent an electric thrill of warmth through the rescuer's own body, restoring his circulation which had begun to chill; and by the time the third traveller was able to walk again, the good Samaritan was in a healthful glow. Together they reached a place of safety; but the man who had tried to save his own life only, perished in the snow, overcome by the deadly cold.

IV. In doing good the right hand should not know what the left hand doeth

Put a seal upon your lips and forget what you have done. After you have been kind, after love has stolen forth into the world and done its beautiful work, go back into the shade again, and say nothing about it. Love hides even from itself. Oberlin was travelling on one occasion from Strasbourg. It was in winter. The ground was deeply covered with snow and the roads were almost impassable. He had reached the middle of his journey, and was so exhausted that he could stand up no longer. He commended himself to God, and yielded to what he felt to be the sleep of death. He knew not how long he slept, but suddenly became conscious of someone rousing him up. Before him stood a wagon-driver, the wagon not far away. He gave him a little wine and food, and the spirit of life returned. He then helped him on to the wagon, and brought him to the next village. The rescued man was profuse in his thanks, and offered money, which his benefactor refused. " It is only a duty to help one another," said the wagoner, " and it is next thing to an insult to offer a reward for such a service ".

" Then," replied Oberlin, " at least tell me your name, that I may have you in thankful remembrance before God ". " I see," said the wagoner, " that you are a minister of the Gospel ; please tell me the name of the good Samaritan ". " That," said Oberlin, " I cannot do, for it was not put on record ". " Then," replied the wagoner, " until you can tell me his name, permit me to withhold mine ".

Service rendered in this spirit will bring glory to God. Therefore, " let your light so shine before men, that they may see your good works, and glorify "—not you (no true Christian desires that)—but " your Father which is in heaven " (Matthew 5. 16).

V. By good works we adorn the doctrine of God our Saviour

Dr. Watkinson says : " There is a piece of music spread out before me. I am told it is magnificent, but as I do not know anything about music I cannot read it ; I simply believe what I am told, namely, that it is a beautiful piece of music. But I hand it to someone who can play. The musician sits at the organ, and with his eyes upon the page sweeps the keys with his fingers. That musician is not making the music : he is not the composer ; but he is adorning the music by interpreting it to me so that I can understand it ". The men and women whose lives are filled with good works are the most practical exponents and interpreters of the music of the Gospel message ; for they apply the spiritual blessings and material benefits of the Evangel to the needs and circumstances of the hour. Thus, Florence Nightingale, spending and being spent on behalf of the soldiers amid the rigours of the Crimea; Mary Slessor, wearing herself out in loving-hearted service to the benighted Africans; Mary Reed, giving her life to the lepers of India, and eventually dying among them, herself a leper: these noble women, impelled to their sacred tasks by a yearning pity for mankind, the burning charity divine, are among the choicest of the gifts with which God has blessed and enriched our poor world. They adorned the Gospel, and were themselves adorned by it (1st Timothy 2. 9, 10). It was in this way that many of the early pagans were won for our Lord. When maligned and persecuted, the Christians did not retaliate, but laid before their persecutors the unanswerable argument of kindly deeds (1st Peter 2. 12). "In the deed," says Cowper, "the unequivocal authentic deed, we find the true argument, we read the heart".

This, after all, is the purpose for which we are left in this world. The very purpose of our blessing is that we may be a blessing to others. Would it be worth our while to construct an expensive machine simply for the purpose of having it run and show its perfection? We construct our machine to accomplish results, to perform work, to produce something that will not only pay its cost but benefit mankind. And so, one great object of God in saving, sanctifying, and boundlessly supplying the needs of His people, is to have them think not of themselves, but of others, and prepare them for every good work.

VI. In good works the propelling power is love

Someone watched a frail nursing sister cleaning the gangrenous sores of wounded soldiers, and said:

" I would not do that for a million dollars ". Without pausing in her work, the nurse said : " Neither would I ". The love of Christ is the great constraining power for such tasks. May we ever remember, too, that

" No works shall find acceptance in that day,
When all disguises shall be swept away,
That square not truly with the Scripture plan,
Nor spring from love to God, nor love to man."

VII. Good works form the practical expression of the Gospel

If, on the one hand, we are exhorted to offer the sacrifice of praise to God continually ; on the other hand, we are urged not to forget to do good and to communicate ; for with such sacrifices God is well pleased (Hebrews 13. 15, 16). If it is true that we are a holy priesthood to offer up spiritual sacrifices acceptable to God, it is equally true that we are a royal priesthood to show forth the virtues of Him Who hath called us out of darkness into His marvellous light ; and good works form the exposition by which the latter form of priesthood is best appreciated by man. Sanctity—holy priesthood (1st Peter 2. 5) ; Dignity—royal priesthood (1st Peter 2. 9) ; find their practical expression in Benignity—doing good (1st Peter 2. 12).

The word about the inhabitants of Meroz—Judges 5. 23—has a stirring message for us all.

" ' Curse ye Meroz ', said the Lord."
" What has Meroz done ? " " *Nothing.*"
" Why then is Meroz to be cursed ? "
" Because Meroz did *nothing* ! "

"What ought Meroz to have done?"
"Gone to the help of the Lord."
"Could not the Lord do without Meroz?"
"The Lord did do without Meroz."
"Did the Lord sustain any loss?"
"No, but Meroz did."
"Is then Meroz to be cursed?"
"Yes, and that bitterly."
"Is it right that a man should be cursed for doing nothing?"
"Yes, when he ought to be doing something."

In contrast to the people of Meroz, we ought to do all the good we can, by all the means we can, in all the ways we can, in all the places we can, at all the times we can, to all the people we can, as long as ever we can. And let us remember that now is the accepted time for the exercise of these sacred ministries. President Lincoln used to say that he had no difficulty in finding men who would shed their last drop of blood for America. His difficulty was to find a man who would shed the first drop! A rich man once said to a servant of God: "Why is it that everybody is always criticizing me for being miserly when they know that I have made provision to leave everything I possess to charity when I die?" "Well," replied the other: "let me tell you about the pig and the cow. The pig was lamenting to the cow one day about how unpopular he was. 'People are always talking about your gentleness and your kindness,' said the pig. 'You give milk and cream, but I give even more. I give bacon and ham—I give bristles, and they even pickle my feet! Still nobody likes me. I'm just a pig. Why is this?' The cow thought for a minute and then said : ' Well, maybe it's because I give while I'm still living ! ' "

Let me conclude by quoting an exhortation which calls us to unwearied well-doing ; an apostolic prayer which shows us where our power lies ; and the verse of a poem which, if translated into action, will make our Christianity a useful and an eminently winsome thing. " Let us not be weary in well doing ; for in due season we shall reap, if we faint not. As we have therefore opportunity, let us do good unto all men, especially unto them who are of the household of faith " (Galatians 6. 9, 10). " Now the God of peace, that brought again from the dead our Lord Jesus, that great Shepherd of the sheep, through the blood of the everlasting covenant, make you perfect in every good work to do His will, working in you that which is well-pleasing in His sight, through Jesus Christ ; to Whom be glory for ever and ever, Amen " (Hebrews 13. 20, 21). So,

"I want, in this short life of mine,
As much as can be pressed
Of service true for God and man ;
Help me to be my best."

(DR. A. B. SIMPSON.)

Chapter XIII

THE BLESSEDNESS OF CHRISTLIKENESS

"NOW thanks be unto God Who leadeth us forth in triumph with the Anointed One, and diffuseth by us a sweet fragrance of Him in every place" (2nd Corinthians 2. 14, Rotherham).

The supreme witness for God in this world is the one whose life is Christlike in spirit and conduct. "To be like Christ," says Henry Drummond; "compared with that, every ambition is folly, and all lower achievement vain." Just as glass may be considered as brilliantly beautiful until we see the fascinating radiance of a diamond, so, when we behold our all-glorious Lord, we are ready to cry out with one of old: "He is altogether lovely".

> "No mortal can with Him compare,
> Among the sons of men;
> Fairer is He than all the fair,
> That fill the heavenly train."

In Mark 3. 14 it is said that the Lord Jesus ordained twelve, that they should be with Him, and that He might send them forth to preach; and in Acts 4. 13 we have an illustration of the effects of that. The officers took knowledge of Peter and John that they had been with Jesus, because these two men of God carried with them the fragrance of the One in Whose presence they had been dwelling. For us to-day who have not access to His physical presence, the whole secret is enshrined in a word which occurs three times in the New Testament; the word *metamorphoomai*. This word is found in Matthew 17. 2, where it is translated "transfigured"; in Romans 12. 2, where it is rendered "transformed"; and in 2nd Corinthians 3. 18, where it appears as "changed". The first of these occurrences shows the pattern *to* which; the second, the principle *upon* which; and the third, the power *by* which, we are transformed. "We all, with open face beholding as in a glass the glory of the Lord, are *changed* into the same image from glory to glory, even as by the Spirit of the Lord" (2nd Corinthians 3. 18). The transformation produces the fragrance. Samuel Rutherford prayed that the Rose of Sharon growing in his heart, might shed its fragrance abroad in his life; and wherever he went, he scattered abroad the perfume of the knowledge of God.

Long years ago the first Protestant missionary to Japan was once brought into touch with members of the royal house of that country. During his furlough in England, he was visited in his rooms one day by some members of the Emperor's family who were touring Europe. They chatted for perhaps an hour and then left. Later in the day another group of Japanese—officials—called. "Oh!" one of them exclaimed, "You have been entertaining royalty here to-day!"

"What makes you think so?" the missionary queried.

"Why, there is a perfume manufactured in our country for the exclusive use of royalty. No one else is allowed to use it, and its fragrant odour is in evidence in this apartment, so that we know you have had royal visitors to-day ! "

Our King has promised not only to visit us, but also to *abide* with us (John 14. 23). Is the fragrance of His presence diffused from us day by day? If so, we shall be following in the footsteps of Paul who said : " For to me to live is Christ ".

" Not merely in the words you say,
Not only in your deeds confessed,
But in the most unconscious way
Is Christ expressed.

" Is it a beatific smile?
A holy light upon your brow?
Oh, no : I felt His presence while
You laughed just now.

" For me 'twas not the truth you taught,
To you so clear, to me still dim ;
But when you came to me, you brought
A sense of Him.

" And from your eyes He beckons me,
And from your heart His love is shed,
Till I lose sight of you, and see
The Christ instead."

There is one other thing which we would do well to note, namely, that a fragrance is the same everywhere. " He makes my life a constant pageant of triumph in Christ, diffusing the perfume of His knowledge everywhere by me " (2nd Corinthians 2. 4, Moffatt). A rose smells as sweetly in the kitchen as in the drawing room ; in the house of business as in the prayer meeting; on the playground as in the sanctuary.

Some years ago a dear friend of mine wrote a poem which he entitled, *The Christian Business Man's Prayer*; but, as its beautiful words may form the heart desire of all the children of God, whatever their sphere may be, I close this section of my little book by quoting them.

" Lord Jesus, in the busy mart,
The hurrying crowd, the anxious strife,
Maintain Thy throne within my heart,
Be Thou to me my very life.

" The wild pursuit of paltry pelf,
The craze and lure of wrong desires,
The world that lives without Thyself,
And all for self alone aspires—

" Let these all leave me undismayed,
Untouched, unstained, by sin or shame,
Calm, and at all times unafraid,
Indifferent quite to worldly fame.

" But filled alone with Thee, my Lord,
And all of Heaven's joy beside,
Thus walk with Thee in glad accord,
And find my Heaven at Thy side.

" One look of love from Thy kind eyes,
One pressure of Thy nail-scarred hand,
Are more than earth's most thrilling prize,
Acclaimed abroad in every land."

EPILOGUE

"Grant Unto Thy Servant"

A holy dissatisfaction with present attainments.

A holy victory over indwelling sin and outward temptation.

A holy faith in the love and power of God my Father.

A holy desire to be a vessel unto honour.

A holy urge in the pathway of loyal service.

A holy interest in all that is for God in the world.

A holy courage to fight valiantly the good fight of faith.

A holy disregard to the allurements of the world.

A holy peace in the midst of stress and storm.

A holy love for all the children of God.

A holy gladness when things depress.

A holy anticipation of the Lord's return from Heaven.